TENNESSEE

A Photographic Journey

TEXT: **Suzi Forbes**

CAPTIONS: **Louise Houghton**

DESIGNED BY: **Teddy Hartshorn**

EDITORIAL: **Louise Houghton and Gill Waugh**

PRODUCTION: **Ruth Arthur and David Proffit**

DIRECTOR OF PRODUCTION: **Gerald Hughes**

CLB 2623
© 1991 Colour Library Books Ltd., Godalming, Surrey, England.
All rights reserved.
This 1991 edition published by Crescent Books,
distributed by Outlet Book Company, Inc., a Random House Company,
225 Park Avenue South, New York, New York 10003.
Printed and bound in Hong Kong.
ISBN 0 517 05304 7
8 7 6 5 4 3 2 1

TENNESSEE

A Photographic Journey

Text by
SUZI FORBES

CRESCENT BOOKS
NEW YORK

The story of Tennessee is one of adventure, music, romance, daring men and spirited Southern belles. It's the land of Davy Crockett, Jack Daniel, Dolly Parton, Elvis Presley and Andrew Jackson.

Of all Tennessee characters, the one who looms largest in American history is Andrew Jackson. It was Jackson who made the American dream a reality for, much as people denied it, the American presidency was held by an elite aristocracy until Jackson changed all that.

Young Andrew Jackson entered the world on March 15, 1767, in a well-to-do farmhouse owned by his aunt and uncle in southeast Tennessee. His father had died several days earlier. By the time Andrew reached the age of fourteen, death had also claimed his older brothers and his mother, all victims of the Revolutionary War.

Hugh, the oldest, gave his life in the battle of Stono. Robert, the next in line, along with Andrew, joined their compatriots to repel the British. Both were captured. Robert was ordered to black the boots of British officers. He stubbornly refused and was struck with a sword. Either his wound or the devastation of smallpox took his life. The boy's mother joined a party of volunteers who went from hospital to hospital nursing the wounded. She caught prison fever and died.

Andrew grew to be a fiesty, adventure-seeking boy who loved to fight and brawl and to gamble on cock fights, horse racing, cards or whether the sun would rise. He was once described as "the most roaring, rollicking, game-cocking, card-playing, mischievous fellow that ever lived."

At seventeen, Andrew decided he wanted to be a lawyer. He joined a class of students under Spruce Macay, a lawyer in Salisbury, North Carolina. Whether he learned much law or not is debatable, but at the end of his studies he set out for Nashville, a small community in the Cumberland Valley. In no time at all, his practice grew to a respectable size. And as Nashville grew, so did the prosperity of Andrew Jackson.

For a time Jackson lived in a boarding house run by Mrs. Donelson, wife of the late John Donelson, one of the founders of the settlements in the Cumberland Valley. Living in the household at the same time was a young Donelson daughter, Rachael. Rachael was married to Lewis Robards of Kentucky, but because of his cruelty to her she had fled back home to her mother. Andrew and Rachael fell in love. It would have been an ordinary love story except that the circumstances of their meeting were to plague them for the rest of their lives.

Lewis and Rachael certainly didn't love one another and Rachael had abandoned Robards. Lewis Robards filed for divorce and in 1791 word reached Nashville that the divorce had been granted. Andrew wasted no time in marrying the lively Rachael.

But the story wasn't over. Two years later, word reached them that Robards was going to file for divorce in Kentucky. There had never been an earlier divorce, and for two years Rachael had been married to two men.

Eventually, the divorce was granted. Another wedding was held to make the Jackson/Robards marriage all tidy and legal. Nevertheless, political enemies used the circumstances of this marriage as a weapon against Jackson for the rest of his life. Despite this, the marriage was happy, content and filled with family. Although the couple never had any children of their own, their home was forever filled with nieces, nephews and children. At one point they gave refuge to an Indian boy who had been orphaned and eventually they adopted a boy of their own.

Married life failed to quell Jackson's spirit of adventure. He was in several duels, resulting in various wounds. By this time he had also become one of the weathiest farmers and planters in Tennessee.

And then the War of 1812 began. Jackson was by now a Senator from Tennessee and a general in charge of the state militia, and it was while he was engaged in a fierce battle with the Creek Indians that he learned of the British invasion just outside New Orleans. He moved his troops to that threatened city in a mere nine days.

The Battle of New Orleans has gone down in history as a most unusual one – and one of the saddest of all time. In the first place, the peace treaty had been signed two weeks earlier, but word hadn't reached Louisiana. That's why this has been called "The Battle that Missed the War." In the second place, the experienced British troops, fresh from the Napoleonic Wars, were to face a polyglot of Americans.

General Jackson was made commander of the United States forces in the South. He faced General Sir Edward Packenham, who brought with him 10,000 crack English soldiers, the most experienced military force in Europe. They frequently bragged that they had "licked Napoleon once a week" during the Peninsular Campaign. These were the same troops that, five months earlier, had marched into Washington unimpeded and burned the White House.

Jackson was in command of a motley crew, quickly organized, and including slaves, dandies, plantation owners, blacks, whites, Indians, backwoodsmen and farmers from Tennessee and Kentucky. There were 2,000 at most and virtually none had fought in a battle before. Furthermore, they had no more than 700 rifles between them. When the Kentucky troops arrived without guns, Jackson angrily shouted, "I don't believe it. I have never seen a Kentuckian without a gun and a pack of cards and a bottle of whiskey in my life."

Jackson received his strongest help from an unlikely source. The pirate Jean Lafitte directed his far flung activities from a spot just outside New Orleans on Barataria Bay. With the outbreak of hostilities, Lafitte offered his men and services to Jackson, who gratefully accepted.

To defend New Orleans, Jackson decided to dig ramparts in a solid line from the Mississippi River to the swamp out on the Chalmette Plain. He felt that the best course of action (especially without guns) was a good defense. His men could use the ramparts as a barricade.

General Packenham was a skilled general. He made a night attack and captured a plantation at the edge of the ramparts. Jackson, never known for his cool, roared: "By the Eternal, they shall not sleep on our soil." And the battle was on.

Not waiting for daylight, Jackson blackened the faces of a small contingent of soldiers and attacked the British with tomahawks, knive and clubs, whooping and yelling all the time. That did the trick. Not knowing how many more heathens might be lurking in the darkness, the British fled, and the interval before they regrouped and attacked again gave the Americans time to finish the ramparts.

Finally, in early January 1815, Packenham launched a full attack. Under cover of fog, the well-formed line of British soldiers marched to drum cadence across the plain toward the

American line. Merely 200 yards from the line, the fog lifted to reveal a solid line of soldiers, fully armed, just waiting for the order to fire. It must have been an awful moment for the British. Jackson gave the command and the report of 500 long rifles shattered the still air. In fifteen minutes the British could take no more. They broke and ran in total disarray.

Packenham reformed his troops and personally led them into that spitting agony again, only to be shot from his horse and killed. Again and again, the scene was repeated. The crack soldiers of the Royal Highland Regiment in full regalia were mowed down, their bagpipes still wheezing. The British lost over 2,000 men; the Americans only seven.

Returning to his beloved Hermitage, his home in Nashville, now as a distinguished general, Jackson resumed the life of a farmer and planter. But not for long. He ran for the Presidency of the United States in 1823 and won the popular vote against John Quincy Adams. In the electoral college, however, Adams won the vote.

The election was barely over when Jackson launched his campaign for the Presidency in 1828. His candidacy was the American dream. It proved that the Presidency of the United States was attainable by the average man.

Yet the campaign turned out to be one of the most vitriolic and vicious in history. Jackson was accused of being a murderer, slave trader, gambler, brawler, cockfighter and an adulterer. The whole messy business of his marriage to Rachael was reported in newspapers and joked about in bar rooms. Jackson, always tremendously protective of Rachael, was furious.

Jackson won the election resoundingly. But the price to his personal life was too high. A few days after the election, Rachael died. The death was listed as due to a cold, but most blamed the brutality of the political attacks. Rachael felt humiliated and ashamed and a liability to Jackson.

As the first President truly "of the people", Jackson invited the "people" into the White House for the reception following his oath-taking. They clambered on the furniture in muddy boots, smashed china and glassware, tore draperies from the windows, knocked waiters off their feet and caused a tremendous commotion. Jackson himself finally escaped through an open window.

Jackson served for two terms as President, but suffered ill health and melancholy the entire time. In 1837 he left Washington and returned to the Hermitage, where he died in 1845.

Jackson s contemporary, Davy Crockett, cut quite a swath through Tennessee and Washington, D.C. himself, He was crude, combative and a legendary Tennessean in his own right. He fought side by side with Jackson in the Indian Wars. In fact, he was such a staunch supporter that he was quoted as saying he would "eat any man opposed to Jackson."

Crockett was not born on top of a mountain, as the hillbilly song says, but at Limestone Creek in Green County. He loved to dress in picturesque buckskins and a coonskin cap. His reputation as an Indian fighter was well earned, but he was primarily the enemy of the land-greedy who wanted to push the Cherokee from their lands, and of the land speculators who threatened the small squatters.

Crockett was known as a yarn spinner. He authored an exuberant autobiography that contained tales of his life in the backwoods, where he claimed he wrestled grizzly bears, and it was punctuated with other extravagent stories, swagger, jokes and lies. He was always ready with a tall tale.

Crockett was elected to Congress by his Tennessee constituency, where he voted independently, serving his conscience first. He and Jackson differed in their ideas about what should be done with the Indians. Jackson believed they should be resettled west of the Mississippi River, and Crockett strongly disagreed. Finally, Crockett's views resulted in his failure to win re-election. In anger, he abandoned his native Tennessee for a new life in Texas. There, in 1835, he fought in the battle of the Alamo, where he lost his life.

It was in the year 1846 that another Tennessee legend was born. His name was Jasper Newton Daniel, but everyone called him Jackie as a child and Jack after the age of seven. As the youngest of ten children, Jack found life on a small farm difficult. He hated being the runt.

On his sixth birthday, with merely a "goodbye" to his favorite sister, he left home and went to live with a next door neighbor, Uncle Felix Waggoner and his wife and two children. A year later, on his seventh birthday, Jack had his first birthday party, an event he talked about for the rest of his life.

Several days after his seventh birthday Dan Call, owner of a country store and whiskey still, called on the Waggoners. He had an idea. Could Jack come live with him and his wife to help Mrs. Call in the store? Jack thought that was a splendid idea and so he moved in with the Calls.

Jack learned to make change at the store and ran errands, but even at seven he pleaded with Dan Call to let him help with the whiskey still. Obviously, he was much too young and the answer was always an emphatic "NO!" And then one morning Jack saved Dan Call's life.

They were walking through a field when the sound of a rattlesnake stopped them in their tracks. It was coiled for a strike straight at Dan Call. Jack raised a stick and slammed it down on the rattler's head with all his might, killing the creature.

Dan Call said: "Jack, you have saved my life. You are already a man in my eyes. From now on you can come to the still house whenever you want, and if you want to learn to make whiskey, I'll teach you the best I know how." Jack was still merely seven years old.

Dan Call knew how to make the best whiskey around. He had a natural outlet, too, by selling it at his store. But then temperance and religion got the best of Dan.

Temperance preachers were common in those days. A woman by the name of Lady Love was traveling from church to church in Dan's valley in Tennessee. She was an evangelist who could stir up a congregation about the evils of stills and whiskey and the men who made and drank it, and she changed Dan Call's life.

When Lady Love moved on, Dan made a proposition to Jack Daniel. He offered the boy, who was now thirteen and who knew more about whiskey-making than anyone else around, the opportunity to buy the business from him on credit. Jack jumped at the chance.

Jack had no trouble making the whiskey; his biggest challenge was finding a new place to sell it. Eventually he found it in Huntsville,

Alabama. Records show that Huntsville had a population of 3,657. The Civil War left the town virtually unscathed and by 1870 the population, including carpetbaggers, muckrakers and scalawags, had increased to 15,527 whites and 15,740 Negroes. When Jack started his selling trips to Huntsville, the year was 1860. He had selected a natural outlet for his product.

Apparently there was no public outcry against whiskey drinking in Huntsville during the war. But certain formalities had to be observed. For one, whiskey could not be sold while police officers were on duty. Precautions were elaborate to get around this requirement.

Jack Daniel bought a two-horse wagon. He loaded it up in Tennessee with jugs of whiskey, covered the whiskey with hay and covered the hay with loose burlap sacks. Then he and a friend rode to Huntsville, where they were obliged to wait until midnight, when they knew the police would be off duty, to enter town. They went from saloon to eating place to grocery store between midnight and early morning selling their wares, leaving again before the police came back on duty.

Jack knew that the most important components of whiskey-making were good, clear water with no iron content, a water temperature ranging from 56o to 60o, and good transportation facilities. He found the perfect combination in the small village of Lynchburg, and moved his operations there in 1866, expanding them considerably.

Then the word went out that the Government was moving in. Did Jack run? Not an inch. In fact, Jack met the Government man, filed for warehouse registration as Jack Daniel Distillery and thus was recognized as the first registered distillery in the United States. From then on, Jack Daniel's Distillery has proudly had government men measuring, gauging and taxing his whiskey.

By 1877 Jack Daniel had the second largest sour mash operation in the state. He was consuming 33 bushels of corn a day and producing 83 gallons of whiskey. At the rate of $2 a gallon, Jack was then making about $116 a day or $3,316 a month (he closed every Sunday). That was a healthy sum for 1877.

Jack just kept improving and improving his

whiskey. Then, one day in 1904, he showed up at the Louisiana Purchase Exposition (St. Louis World's Fair) with two cases of whiskey in tow. He had entered them in a competition that included the biggest names from around the world, including old-established Scotch manufacturers from Europe. There were twenty-four entries in all and the judges were mostly European. Jack Daniel won the Gold Medal "for making the finest whiskey in the world."

Jack Daniel never did marry, but he took several of his brothers' and sisters' sons into the business with him. In 1907 papers were drawn to transfer ownership of Jack Daniel Distillery to Lem Motlow and Dick Daniel, two of his nephews.

Jack Daniel lived to be sixty-five years of age and died in 1911. When he died, however, he was convinced that everything he had worked for was about to vanish. Prohibition was being heralded in state houses, community meeting halls, churches and in Congress. It was only a matter of time.

In 1909 Lem Motlow bought out his cousin Dick Daniel. By this time Lem had also expanded the business. He opened a chain of saloons, operated a brandy distillery and opened several wholesale liquor houses.

In 1910 Tennessee went dry and Lem Motlow was forced to close the operation in Lynchburg. Undaunted, he opened a new distillery in St. Louis, Missouri. That, too, became a huge success but was closed when Prohibition became the national law in 1918.

Repeal of Prohibition came in 1933. That was three years after Jack Daniel Distillery in Lynchburg had burned to the ground and shortly after the still equipment in St. Louis had been sold and ripped out of the distillery there. But even at sixty-five years of age Lem Motlow was a formidable man. He decided to get back into the whiskey business. And he would do it in Lynchburg.

By this time no one knew how to make whiskey with the professionalism of Lem Motlow. Cheap moonshine had proliferated during prohibition as bootlegging became the norm. Now, Motlow would make the first legal whiskey in fifteen years. He set the first mash in 1938 and bottled and sold one-year-old whiskey

a year later. Lem Motlow realized his dream. By the time of his death in 1947, he had rebuilt the Jack Daniel Distillery plant, as well as its reputation.

Tennessee is rightfully proud of Jack Daniel Distillery and the fame and prosperity it has brought to the state. It's equally proud of its majestic and spectacular parklands. The Great Smoky Mountains, in particular, offer some of the most awesome and inspirational scenery in the world. High along the Appalachian Trail, which separates Tennessee from North Carolina, near Chimney Tops, many look across these rolling hills that remind one of ocean waves and wonder: where did these wondrous mountains come from?

The Cherokee Indians have an answer. Legend says that in the beginning all animals and people lived in the sky. There was only ocean below. When the sky grew too crowded, the people sent a beetle to seek a small piece of land in the ocean. The beetle dived to the ocean floor and brought up a speck of mud that grew and grew until the earth was formed. Next, a great buzzard flew down to find a place solid enough for the people to live. His beating wings struck the soft earth and the mountains and valleys of the Smoky Mountains were formed.

The Great Smoky Mountains attract more visitors than any other National Park. Some ten million visitors come every year to view a park of 520,000 acres. Nearly seventy-five percent of those acres are still in wilderness. Travelers may hike the 800 miles of trails, fish the 700 miles of streams, camp in the back-country trail sites or in developed campgrounds. They can canoe on the rivers, bicycle the roads or climb the craggy peaks.

For the nature lover, the variety is spectacular. The park's vegetation is divided into two basic classifications – the heath balds and the cove-hardwood forests.

Local residents call the heath balds by the slang term "laurel slicks," because viewed from afar they appear to be soft, green carpets of meadowland. Up close, it's apparent that they are the opposite. They're actually a thick tangle of rhododendron, laurel, myrtle and azalea. In June these balds are a blaze of pink, white and purple rhododendrons interspersed with the brighter reds and oranges of azaleas and softened by the paler tones of mountain laurel. This is the most popular visitor season, as tourists tumble out of cars to stare at the spectacular beauty.

The cove-hardwood forests, on the other hand, are the remnants of magnificent forests that once blanketed most of the Eastern United States. Here, over eighty kinds of trees, including buckeye, beech, maple, yellow poplar and oak, reach to virgin heights. Below, on the forest floor, magnificent displays of wildflowers compete for attention with the rhododendrons.

Here may be found the delicate beauty of trillium, lady's slippers, lilies and Dutchman's breeches, all in blues, reds, pinks, yellows and whites. On the highest elevations, red spruce and Fraser fir, shrouded in cold fog, seem to touch the heavens.

With so much natural food abounding, it's not surprising that wildlife is plentiful in the Smokies. There are over fifty species of mammals within the park and over two hundred species of birds. That doesn't even count the forty species of reptiles and seventy of fish.

The mammal that has gained the most notoriety, and claims the greatest interest, is the black bear. He's a fearless soul and may willingly pose for a photo just as he hungrily takes a cookie or a finger as a souvenir of his own. There are currently between 400 and 600 black bear in the park. Actually, only about five percent are panhandlers, the rest carry on about their business, far from the tourist crowds.

Bears don't actually hibernate in winter. On sunny days, even in the dead of winter, a visitor may see them emerge from their dens – perhaps in a hollow tree some twenty to sixty feet above ground – and wander around. But they're not looking for anything to eat. In fall they stored up on acorns and hickory nuts and built up a reserve of fat. Then their gastrointestinal apparatus went to sleep for the winter, so they just stopped eating. When spring begins to warm the air, the bears roam with more purpose. At first they eat only newly formed green leaves as they wait for the summer berries to arrive. In summer the black bear is at his best. This is his favorite season and he gains weight again as he stuffs himself on wild raspberries, blackberries, blueberries and huckleberries.

Although the black bear may win the popularity contest, the Smokies have abundant populations of white-tailed deer, raccoons, opossums, wild turkeys, groundhogs, chipmunks and gray squirrels. A very quiet hiker – and a very patient one – may even be rewarded with a glimpse of a red fox or a bobcat, although these are not as common as many other species in the park. Unfortunately, some animals that were once abundant are now virtually extinct. The bison was last seen in the late 1700s, the American elk in the 1840s and the gray wolf about 1900.

If the Smoky Mountains are abundant in wildlife, they are remarkably sparse in human habitation. The first people to inhabit the Smokies were the Cherokee Indians. They called the mountains the "Shaconage" or "the place of the blue smoke" for the deep blue haze that rises mysteriously from the valleys to the summits. They were a peace-loving people and spent their time hunting, fishing, weaving and carving.

It appears that the first white man to visit Tennessee was the Spanish explorer Hernando de Soto, who came in 1540. It wasn't until the mid-1700s that tales of the rich land filtered east to the already-crowded Atlantic states. Soon German, English and Scottish farmers came to settle the land. Their arrival meant the demise of the Cherokee nation. Century-old customs soon gave way to the newer way of life brought by the white man.

One miraculous accomplishment remained to the Cherokee, however. The Cherokee chief, Sequoia, was so impressed by the ability of white men to read and write that he designed an alphabet for the Cherokee nation. Within two years of this feat, nearly every Cherokee could read and write. There was even a Cherokee newspaper called *The Cherokee Phoenix*.

By the mid-1800s, many white families in the Smoky Mountains were in their third generation. These new settlers, just like the Cherokee before them, cleared land, raised crops, hunted game and grazed their few head of livestock. Where two or three families gathered, millwheels were often built to grind corn and rye to serve the community's needs.

Cabins were fashioned of hand-hewn logs,

with split shake roofs. Wide board planks covered the floors. Women prepared the food, carded, spun and wove wool, sewed clothing, tended the vegetable garden and baked. Men farmed, tended the livestock, hunted and fished. It was a self-sufficient, self-reliant existence. In this rather isolated mountain setting, traditions and social customs grew to create the rich heritage of the present-day Appalachian Mountains.

Church and the strong religious fervor it generated was the foundation of life. Church meetings, reunions, baptisms, marriages, gospel singing and funerals drew the close-knit communities even closer. They joined in barn raisings, corn shuckings and quilting parties to provide mutual assistance and companionship. Strong fundamentalist beliefs, however, forbade dancing and fiddle-playing, as these were considered instruments of the devil.

Even so, the natural spirit of these simple, industrious folk showed forth in haunting melodies, hopeful hymns and lonely ballads. They sang while they worshipped, played and worked. Harmonicas, and even fiddles, became a part of this musical tradition.

And then a new element imposed itself on these pure, hard-working people. The vast forests of the Smokies were discovered by the lumber interests that had virtually used up virgin forests further East. In 1901 the Little River Lumber Company purchased 8,600 acres of land. They were followed by other companies which eagerly snatched up the remaining land. During the next twenty years the forests were literally denuded. There was little, if any, concern for the long-range effects.

Where magnificent stands of spruce, fir and yellow poplar once reached to the heavens, the eye saw nothing but ugly stumps. Logs were skidded out by horse, railroads were built and towns sprang up. Sawmills, spewing smoke and steam, were a common sight.

The mountains' former inhabitants helped bring about these changes. The mountain people cut the trees, sold their land to the lumber companies, laid the roads and sawed the lumber. They also sold honey, apples, butter and eggs to the newcomers.

Yet, even though almost two-thirds of the forests of the Great Smoky Mountains were logged, the one-third that remained represented the largest remaining virgin forest in the East. Few people recognized just what that meant, but one man did. His name was Horace Kephart.

Kephart was born in 1862 in East Salem, Pennsylvania. When he was still a child his family moved to an isolated spot in Iowa. He was an only child and spent most of his time reading or making up imaginary adventures.

When he was old enough, Kephart finished his education at Boston University, Cornell and Yale. He married and became the librarian for the St. Louis Mercantile Library. Even though this was a prestigious position, Kephart seemed to become more and more withdrawn.

One day a tornado in St. Louis affected Kephart in a strange way. His nerves were seriously jarred and doctors told him he had to take a rest. Kephart himself described the experience: "...then came castastrophe; my health broke down. In the summer of 1904, finding that I must abandon professional work and city life, I came to western North Carolina, looking for a big primitive forest where I could build up strength anew and indulge my lifelong fondness for hunting, fishing and exploring new ground."

He chose a tiny village in the Great Smokies and it's lucky for America that he did. The area he chose he described as "...the forest primeval, where roamed some sparse herds of cattle, razorback hogs and the wild beasts. Speckled trout were in all the streams. Bears sometimes raided the fields and wildcats were a common nuisance. Our settlement was a mere slash in the vast woodland that encompassed it." Kephart was a writer and he wrote lovingly about his new home. His articles were published and other people learned about this unspoiled land.

Horace Kephart thrived in his new land. But as he watched its destruction by the lumber interests, he realized he had to do something or this entire mountain range would be lost to future generations. He summed up his feelings in 1923: "When I first came into the Smokies the whole region was one superb forest primeval. I lived for several years in the heart of it. My sylvan studio spread over mountain after mountain, seemingly without end, and it was always clean and fragrant, always vital, growing new shapes of beauty from day to day. The vast trees met overhead like cathedral roofs... Not long ago I went to that same place again. It was wrecked, ruined, desecrated, turned into a thousand rubbish heaps, utterly vile and mean."

That was enough for Kephart. He began to think in terms of a national park. Soon, through his writings, national attention was drawn to the cause.

Regrettably, land in the Smoky Mountains was not easy to acquire for a national park. Unlike the Western states, land here was mostly in private ownership. Nevertheless, community programs, individual donations and school drives raised over a million dollars by 1926. In 1927 the legislatures of Tennessee and North Carolina donated two million dollars each. Then, a donation of five million dollars came from the Rockefellers. Still it was not enough. But it all helped and, bit by bit, the lumber barons were bought out.

Finally, in 1934, Congress passed the necessary legislation authorizing full development of the Great Smoky Mountains National Park. Thanks to Kephart and many others who worked tirelessly toward this result, the United States now has a priceless legacy. Within two days' drive of half of the population of the Eastern United States lies a haven – a welcome retreat from the pressures of everyday life. It's a place that people return to again and again – a family place combining beauty, recreation and nature. Thank you, Horace Kephart.

But even as preservationists and environmentalists were striving to preserve one of the world's greatest resources, an event of profoundly different dimensions was taking place just to the West, in the little town of Dayton. It was a hot summer in 1925 and the events taking place here were to reverberate around the world. We know it as the Monkey Trial.

On March 21, 1925 the legislature of Tennessee passed a law making it illegal for any public school teacher "to teach any theory that denies the story of the Divine Creation of man as taught in the Bible, and to teach instead that man has descended from a lower order of animals." This was a direct challenge to biology teachers who routinely used Darwin's *On the Origins of Species*

as one of their teaching aids.

Some schools were outraged. Wasn't this imposing certain dogmatic views on an entire population? They decided to test the new law. A biology teacher by the name of John Scopes admitted he had used such material in a classroom and agreed to participate in the test case. He later testified that every person had the right to "be free to think his own thoughts, to believe as his conscience dictated, not as someone else or the state dictated."

The trial began on July 13th. It might not have caused such a commotion except for several factors in addition to the new law. One was the presence of America's two most famous attorneys. Clarence Darrow was a renowned defense lawyer, religious skeptic, humanitarian and wily debater. He was defending Scopes. William Jennings Bryan – the Great Commoner – was a politician, religious fundamentalist and a silver-tongued orator. He was prosecuting the case for the State.

These two great speakers drew a crowd of reporters unequaled in America. For the first time in history, a Chicago radio station established a nationwide radio hookup to keep its listeners informed about events in the courtroom. H. L. Mencken, the famous Baltimore reporter, covered the event, as did Adolph Shelby Ochs of Chattanooga for his *Chattanooga Times*. Ochs later became head of one of the most powerful publishing dynasties in history – The New York Times Company.

The second reason for the fuss seems to have been the atmosphere in which the trial was conducted. This was no sedate and serious trial. A carnival spirit existed throughout the tiny town and even invaded the courtroom itself. The local soda fountain started selling a Monkey Fizz, townsfolk called the trial "that monkey business," hucksters peddled wares on the courthouse steps, pamphleteers distributed their books, temporary tents were set up on city streets where preachers exhorted the gawking curious about their futures. Mountain men, carrying their huge double-barreled shotguns, came into town for "court day."

Mencken, in particular, penned clever words for his eastern readers about the "yokels" of the region who watched the activities of "civilized persons" for the first time in open-mouthed wonder. He named the region "the Bible Belt", a compliment which the residents, as a whole, accepted gratefully and are proud of to this day.

The trial concentrated more on the clash between religion and science than on the guilt or innocence of John Scopes. The *pièce de resistance* came late in the trial when Darrow took the unprecedented action of calling Bryan to the stand. Questions and answers flew heatedly back and forth. Sometimes shouting, sometimes cajoling, these two antagonists faced each other. The exchange became heated.

"Do you literally believe the whale swallowed Jonah?" asked Darrow.

"Yes".

"Do you believe Moses actually parted the Red Sea?"

"Yes".

Finally Darrow shouted at Bryan: "I am examining you on your fool ideas that no intelligent Christian on earth believes!" With that the judge dismissed court for the day. Next day Darrow entered a guilty plea for Scopes and the trial was over.

For Bryan, the trial was the apex of his long and brilliant career. He was besieged by requests for speeches. He traveled through the countryside giving as many speeches to groups as he could. The sixth day after the trial an exhausted Bryan lay down after the noonday meal in the Dayton home he and his wife had been staying in. He never awoke, passing away in the town where he had waged his last great fight. Bryan had said during the trial: "The Bible is all I need to live by and to die by."

Tennesseans had always been a devout group. It seems the trial made them even more so. One reporter wrote: "More people here are more deeply religious than ever before; and as far as their devotion to the Bible is concerned, they not only haven't gotten further away from it – many of them now carry it in public until the Good Book is as common an everyday sight as a shopping bag."

When it was all over – and it only lasted eight days – the verdict was anticlimactic. John Scopes was fined $100 and the law was allowed to remain on the books until it was finally repealed in 1967. Nevertheless, Tennessee was known for years after as "The Monkey State." In Tennessee stubborn ideas do die a hard death. In 1973 a new law was enacted. It required that equal emphasis be given to Genesis in the classroom, as well as to other theories of man's origins.

Strong beliefs and long-held customs are one of the most admirable Tennessee traits. Yet Tennessee has also witnessed some of the most radical changes of any region of the United States. The landscape was changed radically and dramatically by the Tennessee Valley Authority, for example.

In the 1930s Tennessee was primarily a rural state. Much of it was poverty-striken, with an average personal income of $317 a year. That was merely forty-five per cent of the national average.

Tennessee's land had valuable farming potential, but with few trees, floods frequently ravaged it. There was limited electric power in the state, and some areas had no electricity at all. Hydroelectric projects had met with success in other parts of the United States. Why not in Tennessee?

That idea had already taken shape during World War I in the form of a dam to harness the wild Muscle Shoals rapids in northwest Alabama. Following the war, the project had been abandoned, but, in 1933, President Franklin D. Roosevelt had a proposal for its revival and much more. His historic message to Congress changed the face of Tennessee forever:

"The continued idleness of a great national investment in the Tennessee Valley leads me to ask the Congress for legislation necessary to enlist this project in the service of the people.

"It is clear that the Muscle Shoals development is but a small part of the potential public usefulness of the entire Tennessee River. Such use, if envisioned in its entirety, transcends mere power development; it enters the wide fields of flood control, soil erosion, afforestation, elimination from agricultural use of marginal lands, and distribution and diversification of industry. In short, this power development of war days leads logically to national planning for a complete river watershed involving many States and the future lives and welfare of millions. It touches and gives life to all forms of human concerns.

"I, therefore, suggest to the Congress, legislation to create a Tennessee Valley Authority – a corporation clothed with the power of government but possessed of the flexibility and initiative of a private enterprise. It should be charged with the broadest duty of planning for the proper use, conservation, and development of the natural resources of the Tennessee River drainage basin and its adjoining territory for the general social and economic welfare of the Nation."

Congress agreed with the President. The new legislation was passed. And with its passage, life in Tennessee changed forever. In one fell swoop, Tennessee frontiersmen exchanged their coonskin caps for the hard hats of the TVA.

Soon flood control stabilized the land. A giant stairway of dams and reservoirs tamed the 40,000 square miles of the Tennessee River watershed. Hydroelectric power brought cheap electricity to formerly isolated hill towns, and it brought huge industrial complexes as well. With the new industries came cities and jobs and a shift from a rural way of life to an urban one. By 1974 the TVA estimated that $1.3 billion in benefits could be attributed to its flood control system.

The series of dams and reservoirs brought a mammoth recreational complex as well. The barren land gave way to "The Great Lakes of the South," where boating, swimming, water skiing and fishing are enjoyed on hot summer days.

Dramatic, rapid change often brings negative aspects along with it. The TVA is no exception. Those who were not technically skilled enough to find jobs in the new industrial complexes moved to the cities. A director said: "the TVA had not anticipated the great migration to the city; (the) TVA had a multiple-use resource policy for rural development but no urban policy."

Progress also brought mechanization, congestion and pollution. It traded a slow-paced rural life where stories were swapped around the general store for distance in personal relationships. But it brought prosperity to Tennessee.

The TVA was also indirectly responsible for the most dramatic change ever to take place in the United States. The location was an isolated spot called Bear Creek Valley in East Tennessee. The enterprise was called the Manhattan Project and Tennessee legend says that it had been predicted fully forty years before its inception.

It's difficult to imagine what mountain man John Hendrix had in common with the great German-Jewish scientist Albert Einstein, but one day in 1900 John Hendrix was looking up through the trees when he heard a thunderous voice order him to sleep with his head on the ground for forty days and nights and he would be shown a vision of the future.

Hendrix did as he was told and later he related the following insight into the future:

"I tell you that Bear Creek Valley some day will be filled with great buildings and factories, and they will help toward winning the greatest war that will ever be. Then there will be a city on Black Oak Ridge, the center of everything to be a spot which is middle way between Sevier Tadlock's farm and Joe Pyatt's place.

'Railroad tracks will run between Robertsville and Scarbro," he said. "Thousands of people will be running to and fro. They will be building things and there will be a great noise and confusion and the world will shake." And that's exactly what happened. In 1940, the population of Anderson County was 26,504. By June 1945, a new town had sprung up with a population of its own of 75,000, making it the fifth largest city in Tennessee.

It all started in the early 1940s with a letter from Albert Einstein to President Franklin D. Roosevelt. Einstein felt he could harness the power of the atom. Roosevelt authorized an appropriation of two billion dollars to help him with his research.

The project was cloaked in secrecy from the beginning. It was conceived while Hitler was devastating Europe and Japan was harassing troops in the Pacific. Einstein felt he could make the most powerful bomb the world would ever know. Why was this remote spot in Tennessee selected? The TVA had created a plentiful power supply, the moderate climate of Tennessee would allow year-round construction and an inland location would lessen its vulnerability to enemy attack.

In addition, Lt. General Leslie R. Groves, head of the Manhattan Project said: "Above all, I knew that the labor supply of East Tennessee was of a very high order from the standpoint of work. And, I knew that if we had to use many female operators – and I didn't anticipate as many as we actually required – Tennessee girls would be much more easily trained and would do better work than those of some other sections of the country. The principal reason for this was that the women here were not so sophisticated – they hadn't been reared to believe they 'knew it all.'"

Regardless of the reason, the folks of East Tennessee seemed to welcome the outsiders. A genuine respect grew between the scientists and laborers. Neither could have gotten along without the other. A physicist later said the people "who impressed me most were not the scientists, who knew approximately what they were doing, but the laborers, who didn't... To these laborers – many of them poorly educated men from the local farm country – the intimations of mysterious, invisible danger must have been impressive. Yet I never saw one of them refuse a task or show any uneasiness in exposing himself to the unknown hazard."

The mystery surrounding the project hatched many a wild notion. Most people, scientists as well as locals, had no idea what this project really was. There's the story of a mountain man who asked a scientist if they were building a new Vatican for the Pope. The scientist laughed at the suggestion. To which the mountain man replied: "Well, if you don't know what it is, how do you know it ain't a Vatican?"

Oak Ridge soon resembled a frontier town. Housing was scarce so trailer camps, barracks and dormitories were thrown together. The people inhabiting this strange new town were an unusual breed, too. Theodore Rockwell wrote an article for the *Saturday Evening Post* where he described them. He said: "This project is run almost exclusively by youth, and its influence is felt throughout the area. The whole atmosphere of the work area is that of a university rather than a factory. Almost all the technical men up to the executive positions, are five or less years out of school; the key men are nearly all under forty-five."

Young or old, they got the job done. This experiment in harnessing the atom and purifying uranium culminated in the atom bomb that was exploded with such devastation in the desert of New Mexico on July 16, 1945. Newsman William L. Laurence described it as "... a great green supersun climbing in a fraction of a second to a height or more than eight thousand feet, rising ever higher until it touched the clouds, lighting up earth and sky all around with a dazzling luminosity." It was followed by a wave of intense heat, a thunderous roar and a trembling of the earth.

On December 7, 1941, Japan had launched a disastrous attack on the American naval base at Pearl Harbor in which more than 2,400 Americans were killed. America retaliated and, though battle after battle was fought in the Pacific, in 1945 Japan was still a formidable foe.

On July 26, 1945 President Harry S. Truman called on Japan to surrender or face "the utter devastation of the Japanese homeland." The plea was ignored. So, on August 6, 1945 an atomic bomb was dropped on the city of Hiroshima, killing 68,000 people outright, with a similar number badly burned. That afternoon people who seemed to have survived unharmed died – the first victims of radiation.

It's doubtful that the utter devastation caused by the atomic bomb had been anticipated in Oak Ridge, Tennessee. Certainly it couldn't have been by all those people who didn't even know about the project they were working on. Had they known, many would have refused the jobs. It was now clear that the experiment started on the plains of Tennessee had changed governmental responsibility forever.

General Douglas MacArthur said to the American public by radio: "A new era is upon us... Men since the beginning of time have sought peace... Military alliance, balances of power, leagues of nations, all in turn failed, leaving the only path to be by the way of the crucible of war. The utter destructiveness of war now blots out this alternative. We have had our last chance. If we do not devise some greater and more equitable system, Armageddon will be at our door."

Have we learned? Only the future holds the answer to that question.

As devastating as the results of the Manhattan Project were, the folks of Tennessee returned to the lives they had led with a new knowledge about the world. Tennesseans are a home-loving, family oriented folk. Old ideas are stubbornly held and new ones are treated with skepticism. But the one constant in the life of a Tennessean is his music. Unlike any other area of the country, music permeates all aspects of life in Tennessee.

How did Tennesseans develop such a deep and abiding love of music? Why has Tennessee become the undisputed country music center of the world?

Tennessee mountain music has its core in the ballads of England, Ireland, Scotland and Wales. These first ballads were brought by the eighteenth century British pioneers who pushed into the hills of Tennessee and North Carolina. They brought the haunting tunes with them – stories of broken faith and parted lovers – sad, melancholy songs. The songs were laced with references to long-departed kings, the battles they fought and the ladies they won and lost.

Few of these early songs borrow anything from Negro spirituals, probably because there were few Negroes in the mountains of Tennessee. The music of the mountaineer is the only true folk music ever produced by white men in this country. It has an honesty, dealing with emotions and truths, which reflects popular beliefs.

As the settlers became more Americanized, so did their music. Their songs reflected the lonely, isolated life in the Smoky Mountains, far away from the urban East. The stillness of the hills and valleys created ballads known as "lonesome tunes." They spoke of the dread of Indian attack, and of hunting and fishing, as well as of the struggles of eking out a living in the wilderness.

In 1915, Howard Brockway, an American musical historian born in Brooklyn, visited the Smokies. He wrote:

"We stepped out of New York into the life of the frontier settler of Daniel Boone's time. Here are people who know naught of the advance which has been made in the world outside their mountains. It surpasses belief. In the seventeenth century their ancestors brought the songs from Ireland, England, Scotland and Wales, and they have been handed down orally from generation to generation. Songs that died out in the old country a century ago are still sung every day in the Appalachian region. The statement has been made that among these people one can find nearly all the folk songs ever sung in the British Isles."

Generally speaking, the Smoky Mountain ballad is a narrative. It was formed, with new words and perhaps a new rhythm, by men paying courting visits on their intended or as men gathered around a pot-bellied stove in the general store. An example is *The Girl I Left Behind Me*. This was originally an old Irish air, but was adopted by the soldiers of the Confederate Army, and later by the U.S. Cavalry.

Music was a vital, living part of frontier life. Nearly every home contained a fiddle, "gittar" or "banjer."

For a people whose life is so entwined with their religion, it's not surprising that their music reflects this religious fervor. The early nineteenth century left its imprint on Tennessee's music. These were the days of camp meetings and revivals. Vast groups would gather under a tent in hastily built towns of covered wagons, tents and crude shacks. Fiery evangelists would hold marathon preaching sessions. These sessions were followed by the singing of white spirituals.

The camp meeting spirituals told of the good life after conversion. They differed from regular hymns through their simplicity and heavy use of repetition:

"We'll stem the storm, it won't be long,
The heav'nly port is nigh;
We'll stem the storm, it won't be long,
We'll anchor by and by."

At these camp meetings most songs were sung from memory. Two typical ones born of the camp meetings were *I'm a Lonely Pilgrim Here* and *Let's Go down in the Valley to Pray*. Many were led by the preachers, who could whip the crowd into a frenzy by their impassioned singing. Elvis Presley, the first singer to merge rhythm and blues with a country and western style, once said in an interview:

"I'd play (guitar) along with the radio or phonograph, and taught myself the chord positions. We were a religious family, going round together to sing at camp meetings and revivals, and I'd take my guitar with us when I could."

Camp meetings are not a thing of the distant

past. Their flavor can still be captured at the annual world meeting of the Church of God, in Cleveland, Tennessee. There, a huge choir accompanied by guitar players and violinists leads the congregation in gospel singing.

Even though black spirituals are not the predecessors of white spirituals, they played an important role in shaping the "country and western" music we know today. Nashville's Fisk University made a major contribution. In 1871, a group of eight students calling themselves "The Fisk Jubilee Singers," left on an international concert tour. They sang such classics as *Swing Low, Sweet Chariot* and *Steal Away* for the elite of America, as well as for Queen Victoria. This international attention did much to popularize the Negro spiritual.

In 1873 a man was born who was destined to make another major contribution to the sounds that today emanate from Tennessee. His name was William Christopher Handy. We know him as W.C. and he's recognized as the Father of the Blues.

Handy was born just south of Memphis, and everyone in his family must have discouraged him from pursuing a musical career. His mother disliked the "shout" spirituals in church, preferring the more sedate spirituals, and his father made him return a hard-earned guitar for a Webster's Unabridged Dictionary. Even when Handy attended Fisk University, his teachers instructed the students in classical music, ignoring the important contribution of "The Fisk Jubilee Singers."

Nevertheless, Handy never forgot the haunting songs he'd listened to on the banks of the Tennessee River as a boy. He noted that the black man "sang about everything: trains, steamboats, steam whistles, sledge hammers, fast women, mean bosses and stubborn mules."

At the age of fifteen and without his father's knowledge, Handy paid $2.50 for a used cornet and joined a local band. Shortly after graduation, he struck out for Chicago. He never called Chicago a success but it gave him the traveling bug for the rest of his life. In 1896, Handy was selected to play trumpet in Mahara's Minstrels, which gave him an opportunity to travel the breadth of America. Wherever he went he collected the songs and the moods of the people.

Eventually, Handy formed his own band, playing "for affairs of every description." Then, one night in Cleveland, Mississippi, his group was put to shame by some local folk who were strumming "a kind of stuff that has long been associated with cane rows and levee camps." Handy later wrote: "That night a composer was born, an American composer. Those country black boys in Cleveland had taught me something that could not possibly have been gained from books, something that would, however, cause books to be written."

At the age of thirty-two, Handy moved back to Memphis and took over a large band. He established his band on Beale Street, long associated with gambling, whiskey, women and music. For Handy it was the perfect location.

His big break came in 1909 through an unlikely medium – politics. Handy was hired by ward leader E.H. Crump, who was running for Mayor of Memphis. To bolster the campaign, Handy wrote a tune that he called *Mister Crump*. The song was a blockbuster. All of Memphis was singing it – even dancing to it in the streets. Crump won the election, Handy retitled his song "The Memphis Blues" and tried to have it published. Because it used an entirely new format, publishers all rejected it. Finally, he sold the song to a Denver businessman for $50.00, including all rights. It was another twenty-eight years before Handy himself made any money on his first blues song.

That didn't stop Handy from composing, however. In 1914 he wrote the blues that made him world famous. He called it "St. Louis Blues." Handy never stopped traveling and when he traveled, he wrote, gave lectures and taught. His music merged the music of Southern Tennessee with certain elements of the rest of the country, resulting in its universal popularity.

Handy's music, and that of the rest of the nation, was about to have a boost from another source. In 1920 radio burst on the scene and a year later came records. These two innovations revolutionized the music world. Families who couldn't afford to take the whole family to a minstrel show, could afford a radio. Suddenly, entertainment came right into the home.

Following on in the footsteps of radio came the advent of the radio show. Perhaps none is better known or more loved than the forever popular Grand Ole Opry.

Station WSM in Nashville has been home to the Grand Ole Opry ever since the night in 1925 when seventy-year-old Uncle Jimmy Thompson, a fiddler of local repute, dropped into the station and said he's be glad to play on the air. The announcer, George Dewey Hay, later known as the "Solemn Old Judge," put him in front of the microphone and let him go. An hour later, Uncle Jimmy was asked if he wasn't tired.

"Tired!" he snorted. "Heck, I'm only gettin' started. I played all night last night at a fair."

Listeners loved Uncle Jimmy and wanted more. A string band organized by a country doctor named Humphrey Bate and called the Possum Hunters played the show, as did the Gully Jumpers, the Fruit Jar Drinkers and the Crook Brothers.

The name itself was the result of a radio opera performance in which Walter Damrosch discussed the realism in grand opera. Damrosch was followed on WSM by the Solemn Old Judge, who said: "From here on, folks, it will be nothing but realism of the realest kind. You've just been up in the air with grand opera. Now get down to earth with us in a performance of Grand Ole Opry."

The four-hour show attracted a wide audience. Those who had migrated to cities wanted to retain their musical ties with home and almost from the beginning there was a studio audience. At first the crowd was limited to 150 people. But it just kept growing. Now it's necessary to buy a seat at least a month in advance.

First-rate entertainers vie for the opportunity to perform on stage at the Grand Ole Opry. The show is a combination of country music and comedy, much as the old-time minstrel shows used to be.

Thanks largely to the Grand Ole Opry and to the burgeoning record industry, the music of Tennessee was gaining in popularity and reaching beyond the borders of the state. Boys on the battlefields of Europe or in the Pacific during the Second World War wanted a reminder of their home. They would often quietly sing the old familiar songs in their barracks and foxholes.

In addition, most of the training camps were in the South. When boys from Maine, California and New York heard the "lonesome tunes" on local radio, they found they liked them a lot. When they returned to their homes, they took a taste for mountain music with them.

Soon, big-time dance orchestras played parodies of hillbilly songs, and recordings were made. A pivotal year for music in Nashville was 1946. Three enterprising WSM engineers opened a professional recording studio. The stars of the Grand Ole Opry stayed home to record and a new business was born in Nashville.

By 1949 *Down Beat* magazine reported that hillbilly music was pushing popular tunes out of the limelight. Where a song had sold ten thousand copies a few years earlier, it now sold fifty thousand. Sales were no longer confined to the South, but extended across the nation. Radio stations played mountain music for as much as eighteen hours a day.

One of the earliest stars was Eddy Arnold, a kid from Henderson, Tennessee. He started singing when he was seven years old, so his parents gave him an old Sears, Roebuck guitar. He took four lessons for seventy-five cents each and promptly started playing chords at Saturday night hoedowns. That led him to a six-day-a-week program of playing and singing on Nashville's WSM. He appeared on the Grand Ole Opry and made a movie. By 1944 RCA had signed him to a contract, where he recorded *I'll Hold You in My Heart*, *Bouquet of Roses* and *Molly Darling*. They all hit the top of the charts.

A slim fellow from Maynardsville, Roy Acuff – called by everyone "The King" – captivated the country during the war, too. Roy grew up in the Smoky Mountains, where his father was a Baptist preacher. He never took a music lesson in his life, yet his recording of *Wabash Cannonball* grossed $5,000,000 at seventy-nine cents a record.

Roy wanted to be a baseball player more than anything when he was growing up. And he must have been good, too. He was offered a tryout by the New York Yankees. But while in Florida preparing for his big chance, he suffered sunstroke, which laid him up for two years.

Roy returned home to the farm where he grew up. At a loose end, he remembered the fun he had had following a mule and plow through the stubborn earth. And he remembered the corn shuckings, where a jug of moonshine was hidden in the middle of the pile and the boys shucked to see who could get to it first. Of course, there was music at all times and Roy Acuff was saturated with it.

His "Ma" bought him a secondhand fiddle. As he convalesced, he listened to old records, learned the guitar and sang. He thought he was pretty good. But it took three years for him to convince anyone else of that. Finally, he did get into radio. The audience loved his down-home musical style. He landed a regular spot on the Grand Ole Opry show.

Roy Acuff's songs were the stuff that mountain music is made of. He sang of breaking hearts, lost loves and melancholy. During the Second World War Acuff was named the most popular singer in Europe – surpassing Frank Sinatra. He became country music's first idol and focused attention on the sounds coming from Nashville. Roy Acuff had an impact on all country music and on all the singers who tried to follow in his footsteps.

By the early 1950s the term "hillbilly" was being replaced by "country and western" to escape the derogatory connotations associated with the former. In the early 1900s, the New York Journal had reported that a hillbilly "lives in the hills, has no means to speak of, dresses as he can, talks as he pleases, drinks whiskey when he gets it, and fires off his revolver as the fancy takes him." Now, "country and western" music became a music form in its own right, not just a handed-down version of mountain music.

Perhaps one of the most successful men to follow in Acuff's footsteps was Hank Williams.

Williams was born in 1923 in an Alabama log cabin. He was a volatile man who wrote about deeply felt emotions and was steeped in the traditions of blues and country. He inserted the cry of a whippoorwill and the whine of a midnight train into his songs. When he played for the first time before the audience at the Grand Ole Opry in 1949, he brought the house down. The audience pleaded with him for encore after encore. That night remains one of the most memorable in Opry history.

Williams' greatest contribution to country and western music was not so much his singing, however, as his writing. He was the first country composer to have his songs recorded by national pop stars. *Your Cheatin' Heart* became a hit for Joni James. *Cold, Cold Heart* by Tony Bennett and *Jambalaya* by Jo Stafford. Tragically, Williams died at the age of twenty-nine in an automobile crash.

Jo Stafford became a popular hit with her rich, high voice. Her sophisticated dance song *Temptation*, hit the top of the pop charts, too, and Dinah Shore, a native of Tennessee, changed the European waltz *Forever and Ever* into a hillbilly hit. Finally, such hits as *Good Night, Irene* and *The Tennessee Waltz* catapulted country music into the national mainstream. *The Tennessee Waltz* sold an unprecedented five million recordings in a little over a year.

There's little doubt that the roots of rock and roll stem from country and western music. And the undisputed king of this new musical style was a boy from Memphis named Elvis Presley. Acceptance of Presley was not immediate, however. In fact, the syndicated television critic John Crosby said Presley was an "unspeakable, untalented and vulgar young entertainer." He asked: "Where do you go from Elvis Presley, short of obscenity – which is against the law?"

Actually, a radio station engineer, Sam Phillips, probably had more to do with the emerging rock and roll style and the recognition of Presley's talent than anyone else. Phillips entered the recording business by supervising recording sessions with local blues singers and leasing the masters to independent companies. He then formed his own independent recording company, Sun Studios.

The story of the first Phillips/Presley meeting is the stuff legends are made of. Presley had gone to a studio at Sun to cut a record for his mother's birthday. Phillips heard him and asked him to cut a record using proper accompaniment. They mixed various sounds and styles until Phillips was finally satisfied. That first record became a local hit called *That's All Right*.

Presley said of that meeting: "Mr. Phillips said he'd coach me if I'd come over to the studio as often as I could. It must have been a year and a half before he gave me an actual session. At last he let me try a western song – and it sounded terrible. But the second idea he had was the one that jelled."

"'You want to make some blues?' he suggested over the 'phone, knowing I'd always been a sucker for that kind of jive. He mentioned Big Boy Crudup's name and maybe others too. I don't remember.

"All I know is I hung up and ran fifteen blocks to Mr. Phillips' office before he'd gotten off the line – or so he tells me. We talked about the Crudup records I knew – *Cool Disposition. Rock Me, Mama, Hey Mama, Everything's All Right* and others – but settled for *That's All Right*, one of my top favorites."

Each recording Presley made for Sun was more popular than the last. Soon, he moved on to RCA records and signed a long-term movie contract.

It's hard to imagine that any performer in history has enjoyed a longer and more sustained popularity than Presley. Yet, throughout his popularity, he maintained his Tennessee ties, returning frequently to Memphis, where the religion he learned as a child continued to shape his life.

It's not an accident that so many great Americans have their roots in Tennessee. A blend of hard work, religious conviction and rugged individualism seems to result in greatness here. Tennessee, with its unspoiled beauty, its mountains and streams, plains and meadows encourages creativity, fame and distinction. Lucky is the child born in Tennessee. His opportunities are unlimited.

Previous page: beautiful rural Tennessee. Mud Island (these pages) in Memphis is a fifty-acre celebration of the Mississippi which is run by the City and open all year round for the enjoyment of visitors, who arrive via the pedestrian walkway or the monorail (below left). The entire length of the Mississippi from Cairo, Illinois, to New Orleans is replicated to scale in a five-block-long concrete model (left) called the "River Walk," which includes every bridge and meander in its course. It also boasts a beautiful silver-flushed fountain (below).

The paddlesteamer and the Mississippi River are bound by a long association of mutual dependency; the first steamboat to ply the waters of the "Ol' Man" was launched in 1811. Ten years later transport on the rivers of the South had experienced a revolution and the great ships were being produced just as fast as they could be. Towns like Memphis sprung up in some profusion along the banks of the Mississippi and prospered in the new age brought about by the steamboat. Many gracious craft (these pages and overleaf) with nostalgic names work as pleasure boats today.

33

Downtown Memphis is set out in spacious, carefully lit blocks and offers such high-class accommodation as the Holiday Inn Crowne Plaza (left), which has exceptional convention facilities as well as restaurants, bars and a health center. The Mid-America Mall (above left) is close to the Wolf River, spanned by the intricate steel lacery of the Interstate 40 bridge (above).

The nine hundred miles of the Mississippi River reproduced at "River Walk" (these pages) on Mud Island are in places narrow enough to step over, or deep enough to splash in, and there are even islands upon which to sit. The Mud Island project saved the ignobly named island, which lies between the Wolf and Mississippi rivers, from destruction by city planners.

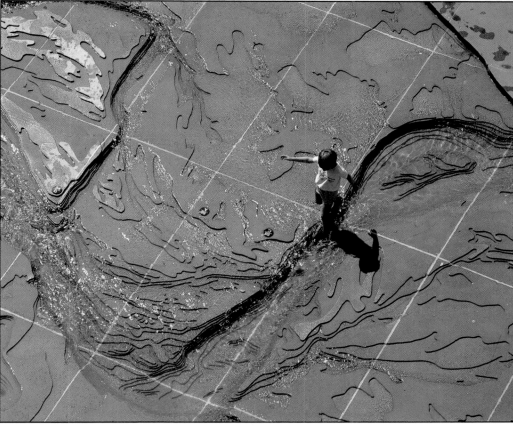

Beale Street in Memphis has an important place in music history, for it was here that the blues were first developed. The cafés, saloon bars, honky-tonks and dance halls that line the famous street (these pages) today keep up the tradition and are a mecca to purists of the art.

"Graceland," the one-time home of Elvis Presley, has been open to the public since 1982, five years after the premature death of this great star. A legend in his own lifetime, Elvis is by no means forgotten by his fans, who regard the handsome house (above) outside Memphis as a shrine. The Meditation Gardens (facing page) are a place of quiet contemplation for followers of the King.

43

The Belle Meade Plantation (these pages) in Nashville will be familiar to those with an interest in Thoroughbred racing and breeding. It was here that Iroquois, who in 1881 became the only American-bred-and-owned horse ever to have won the English Derby, stood at stud. The house itself is a Greek Revival Mansion furnished in keeping with its 1853 construction and hung with many notable equine oil paintings and portraits of the Harding/Jackson family.

Memphis is situated in the extreme west of Tennessee on the bluffs above the Mississippi River near the state's borders with Arkansas and Mississippi. Memphis (these pages) was settled in 1819 on land previously inhabited by Chickasaw Indians, but its founders – Andrew Jackson, James Winchester and John Overton – liked the look of the place and by 1826 it had been incorporated as a town. Memphis has had its hard times, including a cholera epidemic in 1878 so severe that it caused the town's political structure to collapse and forced the surrender of its charter. But today it is the seat of Shelby County and a busy commercial center.

47

The foyer of the Peabody Hotel (left), one of the most prestigious hotels in Memphis, harmoniously combines stately elegance with comfortable informality. The Magevney House (top) on Adams Avenue is also comfortable and informal. Built around 1836 it is the oldest home in the city and exemplifies how life was lived in the early days of settlement. Higher up Adams Avenue in the Victorian Village District is the Mallory-Neely House, in which Miss Daisy's room (above) is most enchanting.

Fontaine House (these pages) on Adams Avenue in the Victorian Village District in Memphis was built in the Queen Anne style in 1890 and is fully furnished with Victoriana. The illusion of stepping back into a bygone era is enhanced by the presence of figures in period costume.

Chucalissa Indian Village south of Memphis is an educational place to visit. The original site upon which the recreated village stands was settled about 1,000 A.D., from which time many of the artefacts on display date. The project was originally intended as an off-campus facility for the department of anthropology of Memphis State University, but it is now a pleasure to all.

Casey Jones, the legendary railroad engineer and Old South hero, is buried in Jackson (above) and his home there (facing page) has been made into a museum. To many, the life of Casey Jones is less familiar than the circumstances of his death, but the museum's colorful exhibits serve to put that to rights. Everyone is, of course, familiar with the folk song he inspired.

Fort Donelson National Military Park (left and below left) is the site of the first significant Union victory in the Civil War. The visitors' center exhibits details of the fighting on that 16th day of February 1862, and many battle defenses remain intact. Davy Crockett's home (below) in Rutherford provides a fascinating glimpse into the lifestyle of the man who became such a legend.

Opryland USA in Nashville is a unique spectacle, being the only musical show park in the entire United States. There are no less than twelve shows on offer here in this 120-acre complex, but music isn't the only attraction – there are gardens, shops, amusements and rides too, so all the family are assured of a good day out at Opryland. Overleaf: Nashville's Music Row.

Nashville boasts much in the way of impressive architecture and public buildings, including the War Memorial Building (above) and Tennessee State Capitol (right). The Capitol, an imposing Greek Revival structure, is elevated on a hill overlooking the city and is the work of William Strickland. Overleaf: the bridge at Paris Landing, silhouetted against a sunset sky.

The city of Clarksville (these pages) was named for General George Rogers Clark, a leader of Patriot forces against the British in the Revolutionary War. It is a picturesque city of great character and charm with many nineteenth-century buildings and a fifteen-acre historic district. Clarksville's early wealth was made as a tobacco port, the area being famous for its fire-cured leaves.

Below: a somber sky looms heavily over Stones River National Cemetery. The Stones River Battle was one of the bloodiest clashes of the Civil War. Both sides claimed victory when the fighting on the battlefield (below right) ended on January 2, 1863, but, though losses were comparable, it was the Unionists that held Murfreesboro. Right: the Cannonsburgh Pioneer Village in Murfreesboro. Overleaf: nearby Burgess Falls.

The Tennessee Technical University in Cookeville is a prestigious seat of learning with elegant campus buildings (above) and grounds. The collection of buildings at Rugby is a mixture of originals and reconstructions of what once formed a Utopian colony founded in 1880 by the English author Thomas Hughes. Its Episcopal Church (right) is still in regular use.

The community of Rugby was established as a place where the younger sons of the English gentry, who, because of their late birth, would not inherit the family estate, might learn the practical skills of farming. Its founder was a social reformer who protested that upper class parents "would rather see their sons starve like gentlemen than thrive in a profession that is beneath them."

Colditz Cove State Natural Area (these pages) is part of Tennessee's South Fork Country, an area rich in natural beauty shaped by the waters that drain its huge upland plateau. Tiny streams of rainwater form high up on the plateau and then gather volume and force on their downward course through rockpools and over precipices such as Northrap Falls (above). Right: the wooded scenery surveyed from above.

La Follette (left), near Norris Lake in eastern Tennessee, is unceremoniously bisected by the five lanes of Highway 25W, busy with trucks and cars all day. Vehicles of a different kind are found on display in the Abraham Lincoln Museum (above) in Harrogate, along with a quarter of a million other items relating to the life of the sixteenth president. Top: Pinnacle Overlook on State Highway 63.

Allandale (left) in Kingsport is the very essence of Old South elegance: perfectly proportioned and graceful in style. Bristol Caverns (below and bottom) are full of dramatic dripstone formations and underground pools. The labyrinth of caves and tunnels was once used by the Indians to provide secret approach and escape routes during their raids on early settlers.

In east Tennessee near Johnson City stands Rocky Mount (above and right), the oldest original territorial capitol in the United States. A two-story building made of white oak logs, it was built in 1770 by William Cobb, and at that time was one of the area's grandest homes. Today it is a living history museum where one may walk back in time to the eighteenth century. Top: restored Fort Watauga and (overleaf) Main Street in Jonesboro.

83

The Smoky Mountains are the subject of songs, poems, books, dreams — even people who have never seen them will tell you how beautiful they are. And they are. Views from (left) the Newfound Gap Road and (below) the Morton Overlook are particularly stunning.

Great Smoky Mountains National Park (these pages and overleaf) is a glorious natural wildlands sanctuary with over nine-hundred miles of walking trails. Rivers, streams, falls, mountains, valleys and forests combine to create a landscape of great beauty which is both remote and accessible. Above: a brook beside Roaring Fork Road, (above right) a view from Morton Overlook, (right) walkers on Chimney Tops Trail and (overleaf) forest splendor.

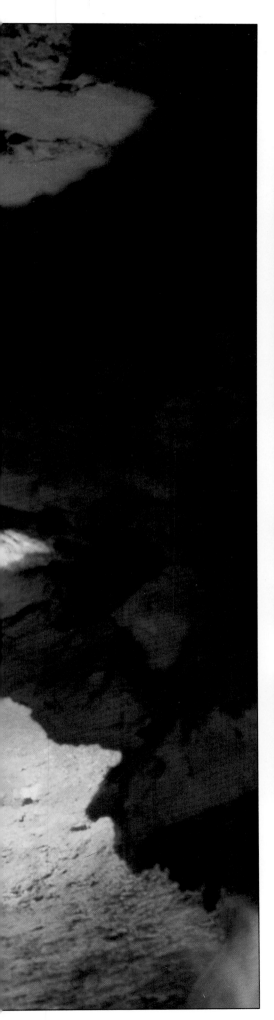

Gatlinburg (above) is an extremely popular mountain resort with a seemingly endless supply of accommodation. Ideally suited for the Smoky Mountain explorer, the town also has attractions of its own, including a wax museum and space needle. The Tuckaleechee Caverns (left) near Townsend provide another interesting visit in Tennessee, the state of contrasts.

Pigeon Forge (above), which lies just north of Gatlinburg, is a colorful resort town in the Smoky Mountains. An evening chairlift ride up Crockett Mountain (facing page) at Gatlinburg is a magical experience and a great way to see the Smoky Mountains.

Tucked away in the depths of Smoky Mountains National Park is Cades Cove, a community of quaint old buildings that supported 685 settlers back in 1850. Gregg Cable House (above left and above), built in 1879, is probably the oldest frame house in the settlement. Cable Mill (left) was used for the grinding of corn and powered a sawmill. Overleaf: the Old Mill at Pigeon Forge, where grain has been ground since 1860.

Knoxville was settled in 1786 by James White, a former captain in the Continental Army who had come in search of land to claim as offered by Congress to encourage recruitment. He was soon joined by other claimants and the name Knoxville was chosen to honor Henry Knox, President Washington's Secretary of War. The modern city (above left) looms high over such historical sites as the Great House (above and left) of White's Fort.

The Blount Mansion (these pages) and its gardens appear just as they did in the eighteenth century. Built in 1792, the mansion served as home to Territorial Governor William Blount, described by an historian as "certainly one of the greatest single forces in the politics of the Southwest, if not the greatest ..." Open to visitors year-round, his home in Knoxville is an educational place to visit.

Fort Loudoun State Historic Area (below) stands on the edge of Tellico Lake near Sweetwater. Built by the British in 1756, the fort was abandoned just four years later when, after a breakdown in British-Cherokee relations, the garrison was effectively forced out by the Indians. The American Museum of Science and Energy (remaining pictures) at Oak Ridge is full of exhibits detailing ancient and modern methods of energy production.

The National Cemetery (above left) in Chattanooga holds the graves of the Unionists who died in the Civil War battles in the surrounding area. By the year 1865 the cemetery contained more than 12,000 graves. The men of New York who fell in the battles at Chattanooga are commemorated by a handsome monument (left). Cravens House (above), on the slopes of Lookout Mountain, was rebuilt after suffering extensive damage in the Civil War, when it was used as a field hospital.

The downtown area of Chattanooga (these pages and overleaf) lies on land hard won through spilling the blood of Indians in the eighteenth century and that of thousands of Civil War soldiers in the nineteenth. So much was sacrificed for the town christened Chattanooga (which is said to be a corruption of an Indian word meaning "pointed rock") because of its sheltered valley location on the Tennessee River and the access it gives to the Deep South.

BATTLE OF CHATTANOOGA, 2ᴰ DAY, NOV.24,

Below: the Chattanooga Choo-Choo, a national institution at the complex of the same name in Chattanooga which includes restaurants, shops and gardens. The train that Glenn Miller made familiar to all the world is held dear in the hearts of Tennesseans. The Tennessee Valley Railroad Museum keeps up the tradition of steam travel, operating authentic old locomotives with authentic locomotive drivers (left).

Lookout Mountain stands 1,500 feet above Chattanooga, affording extensive views (right) of the city, river and surrounding countryside. A vantage point taken by the Confederates during the Civil War, the mountain proved to be no ally, however, as such is its steepness that guns atop it were unable to damage the enemy on its slopes. Deep inside the mountain is Ruby Falls (above), a 145-foot-high waterfall reached by elevator.

Tennessee is famous for its dramatic scenery, and for good reason. Buzzard's Roost (left) justifies that fame and Fall Creek Falls (overleaf) backs it up.

The world-famous Jack Daniel's whiskey is made at Lynchburg, and matured in American white oak barrels (left) that have been charred on the inside. The rock bridge (below left) at Sewanee is an entirely natural wonder. Below: Falls Mill at Belvedere.

These pages: the home of President James K. Polk in Columbia, typical of mid-Tennessee architecture at the beginning of the nineteenth century. Simple in architectural style, it represents the kind of functional abode suitable for a frontier family of the time. Built in 1816 by the eleventh President's father, the house has been made a National Historic Landmark and contains much of its original furniture.

Shiloh National Military Park (above and top), eleven miles south of Savannah, is a lasting tribute to those who died in the Civil War battle around Shiloh church on April 6 and 7, 1862. Of the 110,000 troops engaged in the conflict more than 20,000 were killed or wounded. The natural bridge (left) at Waynesboro is another of the wonders that go to make Tennessee such a special place, as is Pickwick Landing (overleaf and following page), a State Park near the Alabama border.

INDEX